This book is dedicated to all who find Nature not an adversary to conquer and destroy, but a storehouse of infinite knowledge and experience linking man to all things past and present. They know conserving the natural environment is essential to our future well-being.

YOSEMITE

THE STORY BEHIND THE SCENERY®

Yosemite National Park, *located in central California, was established in 1890; it preserves Yosemite Valley, giant sequoias, other forests, and High Sierra wilderness.*

by William R. Jones

William R. Jones has been active for many years as a career professional in the interpretation and planning programs of the National Park Service. A graduate of Stanford University, with major studies in geology, Bill has a broad background in natural history, park management, and conservation. His expert knowledge and fine appreciation of Yosemite, one of our oldest and best-loved national parks, were gained through the ten years he served there as park naturalist.

Front cover: Upper and Lower Yosemite Falls; photo by Jeff Gnass. Inside-front cover: Tuolumne River cascade; photo by David Muench. Title page: Mule deer; photo by Frank S. Balthis. Pages 2/3: Yosemite Valley and Cathedral Rocks; photo by David Muench.

Edited by Mary L. Van Camp. Book Design by K. C. DenDooven

Eighth Printing, • Revised Edition. 1989

*T*ucked away from the mainstream of civilization, an incomparable parkland lies, encompassing in its vast expanse a magnificent but intimate valley; huge granite domes and waterfalls that seem to spring from the sky; soaring, white-capped peaks and forests that speak to us of the primeval: Yosemite is a panorama of natural beauty that "cleanses and warms like fire" yet calms and soothes like balm.

Yosemite! Its cliffs are so high that the first explorers to set eyes upon them could not begin to calculate their heights; its landmark Half Dome is so distinctive that its shape is recognized throughout the country; some of its giant sequoias are so old that contemplation of their great ages strains man's concept of time; and its High Sierra wilderness is so remote and so vast that no one has ever seen it all.

People from every corner of the United States—and the world—travel to this park in central California to gaze upon these attractions and marvel. And well they might, for all these features are truly awesome. But there is another, less prominent dimension to the Yosemite land-scape—and that is the infinite *variety* that the park encompasses.

Four distinct seasons contribute to this diversity, providing weather that ranges from the sunny days of summer, in which the sounds of birds and free-flowing streams blend in tuneful harmony, to the snowy, quiet days of winter, in which the valley is sometimes locked in snows so deep that only a few venture in to enjoy its pristine beauty. Also enhancing the landscape is a dramatic change in topography that occurs within a couple of vertical miles: In a day's time, one can move from a warm canyon bottom to a 13,000-foot elevation, in sight of Mount Lyell and its icy glaciers.

The first view of Yosemite Valley—for its original non-Indian discoverers and for modern visitors.

With such astonishing variety, how could anyone fail to find something in Yosemite that pleases? If in autumn Bridalveil Fall is not at its boisterous springtime best, it is still a remarkable sight, as its narrowed column sways to the side and separates into comet-shaped drops that are flung outward on the wind, so that the water seems no longer to *fall* but to hang suspended in a graceful, gravity-defying dance. If the solitude that one may crave is lacking on the floor of Yosemite Valley in the frenetic activity of summer, it can surely be found in the northern park wilderness. Then, if the rock slopes of the high country begin to seem *too* remote, one can return to the Sierran forests, to enjoy the soothing companionship of the elegant sequoia giants, the world's largest living things.

The truth is that the range and variety of Yosemite is too great for anyone to comprehend in a single visit, a time in which our thoughts are swept from the massiveness of El Capitan and the Sierran peaks to the delicacy of the tiny seedlings from which the giant sequoias grow. Faced with so much overwhelming evidence of nature's complexity, one cannot help but feel the wonder of the forces that can create such beauty and diversity.

It is this spirit of wonder that leads us to explore and investigate the marvelous detail that makes up the world of Yosemite...

A Valley is Carved

The cliffs of Yosemite Valley are sheer, near-vertical walls that rise upward for more than half a mile. As we contemplate their massiveness and that of the majestic domes whose crowns are blazoned on the blue sky overhead, questions as old as man crowd into our minds. How did the land get that way? What forces were at work here to produce such a magnificent scene? Why did *this* valley—Yosemite Valley—come to be carved in solid granite?

The spectacular landscape here has often been referred to as "the incomparable valley." But there are other valleys that rival its splendors.

Just north of Yosemite Valley, and still within the park, Hetch Hetchy Valley on the Tuolumne River is so similar that it is sometimes called the "Tuolumne Yosemite." Outside Yosemite National Park, but still in the same mountain range (the Sierra Nevada) are the magnificent valleys of the San Joaquin, Kings, and Kern rivers. And one might consider also the valleys of Alaska, Switzerland, and Scandinavia, including the ocean-level fiords. All these are comparable valleys and may indeed be rivals, but none can be said to *surpass* Yosemite Valley. (Could there be one that lies buried beneath the ice of Greenland, or perhaps Antarctica, that *does* ?) Yosemite, then, while not basically different from these other valleys, is a classic—and simply the most spectacular valley so far discovered.

That it is not a one-of-a-kind has not always been understood by geologists, however. Josiah Whitney apparently did not understand; in 1865

LARRY ULRICH

Sentinel Rock, a familiar valley feature, allows us to gauge the immense depth of the glaciers that once filled the gorge to its brim and overtopped even this high formation. The ice pared the vertical face along a master crack; today rock fragments continue to loosen and fall into the valley below.

Standing above the Merced River, the El Capita rock formation ranks among the tallest unbroke cliffs in the world. Made of a tough granite, it ha resisted cracking. Its massive valley-side face repelled glaciers so thick they nearly covered i crown. Thus, geological history reveals th evolution of scenery—and also of renowne climbing routes, for skilled rock climbers are ofte seen ascending this rock's near 3,000-foot profil

The High Sierra, source today of water for Yosemite Valley's waterfalls, was once the source of ice for glaciers that descended from here to carve the valley cliffs. This entire region was a zone of snow accumulation during the Ice Age. In fact, when the Ice Age was at maximum, only the tops of the highest peaks stood as islands above a vast sea of white. Although much snow still falls in the High Sierra, now virtually all of it melts during the summers and only tiny glacierets and a few ice fields occur in peak shadows.

he "explained" the origin of Yosemite Valley and concluded that Half Dome had been "split asunder in the middle, the lost half having gone down in what may truly be said to have been 'the wreck of matter and the crush of worlds,'" in which the bottom just "dropped out," producing the "exceptional creation" that is Yosemite Valley.

Whitney's explanation was accepted by most people at the time, but among the doubters one was notable: John Muir engaged the argument head-on, stating, "the bottom never fell out of anything God made" and theorizing a glacial origin instead. In rebuttal Whitney dismissed such arguments as the daydreaming of a "mere sheepherder...an ignoramus." (Muir had not yet won his eminent reputation as a naturalist; at that time he was new to California and his longest employment there had been as a shepherd and sawmill operator.) Whitney continued to attack the "glacial theory" as late as 1874 in his *Yosemite Guidebook.*

Today geologists accept the evidence that Muir eventually gathered to support his theory, but they are still studying other aspects of the origin of Yosemite and are at work mapping its rocks, dating its minerals, and probing underneath it at the root of the Sierra Nevada. Gradually, answers to old questions are being found, but in the process new questions continually present themselves.

One of these puzzles concerns the origin of marine fossils that are present in the rocks at the Sierra Nevada crest on the east side of the park, rocks that now lie at 13,000 feet above sea level yet are held solidly within strata that were clearly laid down in the ocean. Such rocks are also prevalent along the western boundary of the park, and there is even a thin, discontinuous band in the central part, crossing Yosemite Valley in a north-south direction at Sentinel Dome and extending to Mount Hoffmann and Glen Aulin. Were these rocks raised up from the sea? Did Yosemite and the entire Sierra Nevada range, some 400 miles long, rise all at one time?

A Shifting World

One of the most fascinating of the theories that have been presented by geologists is the *plate tectonics* theory, now widely accepted, which holds that the sea floors are spreading apart at rift lines in the ocean basins (where new rock welling up from below replaces that spreading away), moving crustal plates of the earth and causing the continents to drift. Massive global forces thus produce the broad relief features that are exhibited on the surface of the earth—the depression of ocean trenches, the stabilization of flat plains and shallow seas, and the raising of continental mountains.

Some 500 million years ago (the earliest time that we know about anything in the Yosemite region, rocks and fossils of that era having left a record for our information), a shallow sea stretched over what is now eastern California and western Nevada. Material that washed in from land areas adjacent to this sea and erupted into it from volcanoes continued to be deposited over a vast period of time that lasted until about 100 million years ago.

The arresting form of Half Dome, Yosemite's world-famous landmark, causes many viewers to ponder—as did the geologists of more than a century ago—the intriguing question of how this monolith came to have such an extraordinary shape. From this angle, the cleavage of its face helps reveal its origin.

JEFF GNASS

9

Granites of the Sierra Nevada formed from 220 to 80 million years ago. They cooled miles below the surface from molten rock. Near Tenaya Lake, a "vein" on Pywiack Dome shows how cracks may form and then be "healed" by later intrusions. Deep erosion has removed the overlying earth, and the crystalline rock is now visible, revealing these wonders of our inner planet.

This was the pattern of events in the comparatively stable, shallow continental sea that lay just east of what is now Yosemite. In fact, during that period the Yosemite region itself was not even on the continent; it was located to the west on the continental shelf and under the surface of the ocean.

From about 200 to 80 million years ago, massive slabs of rock from the sea-floor plate moved toward the continental plate. The heavier oceanic rocks were dragged downward under the continental rocks, a process known as *subduction.* At the same time the sea-floor plate was moving northward in relation to the continental plate, a long-standing regional trend. Some pieces of the sea-floor plate stuck against the continental mass, but most of these heavier rocks traveled deep under the continental edge into the earth. These

former oceanic sediments and volcanic deposits gradually descended to such a depth that, as temperature and pressure increased, they recrystallized into harder metamorphic rocks. Some got so hot they simply melted.

The rocks below Yosemite turned to fluid in at least three pulses during an otherwise almost continuous sequence of melting at changing localities. The first occurrence caused granite to form 200 million years ago in what is now the eastern part of the park; some of these rocks are now exposed at Tioga Pass and Lee Vining Canyon. The second pulse occurred nearly 140 million years ago in what is now the western part of the park, when most of the granites in the Sierra Nevada foothills and western Yosemite Valley were produced. The third pulse occurred about 85 million years ago in what is now the center of the park, forming the granite at the head of Yosemite Valley (such as Half Dome) and in Tuolumne Meadows.

Each melting pulse lasted 10 to 15 million years. And, due to varying chemical components and differing cooling environments, each pulse produced distinct kinds of granites—with characteristic minerals, textures, and colors—and some near-duplicates.

Where two granite masses came into contact, the older, solid one often would crack. Pressure within the younger, still-fluid rock then injected material into the cracks forming in the older rock, leaving tabular sheets when cooling was completed. If the older and younger rock contrasted much in color or texture, the basis was laid for the vein-like or mosaic patterns we see at the surface now that erosion has produced visible cross-sections of these contacts.

JEFF GNASS

Exfoliation is the process by which rocks expand outward as they release the latent pressure stored within them when they formed deep within the earth. The rocks crack in layers parallel to the surface, aiding in shaping the land.

The deep red color of rocks at Ellery Lake, near Tioga Pass (eastern park entrance), contrasts with the pale gray of granite on the cliff wall beyond. When molten Sierra Nevada granites intruded softer, layered sediments and volcanic rocks, they transformed or "metamorphosed" them into harder, more deeply colored rocks like these.

The granite solidified perhaps five miles below the surface of the earth, probably underneath a mountainous region of volcanoes, lava flows, and ash deposits formed above the intruding granite, much as in today's Cascade Range of Washington, Oregon, and northern California. The ancestral volcanic mountains of the Sierra Nevada began eroding slowly, and then the sedimentary and metamorphic rocks formerly underneath them began to erode. Finally, by 65 million years ago, some of the deep granite was exposed at the earth's surface. (We know this because fragments of Sierra Nevada granite, which must have been eroded from rocks at the surface, are found west of the range in sedimentary deposits of that early time.)

At about 15 to 25 million years ago, the pattern of movement at the boundary between

1. Yosemite Valley's Merced River has not always had a deep gorge for its bed. Once it had no rapids and flowed over a land of rolling hills and shallow tributary streams.

2. Then major forces in the crust of the earth forced the Sierra Nevada to rise higher. The increased steepness caused the Merced, and other streams, to run faster. Thus they eroded their valleys more deeply.

4. Glaciers flowed down the Merced River, filling Yosemite Valley to its brim and smoothing off projecting ridges. The glaciers also carried away the floors of side canyons, later causing tributary streams to "hang" as waterfalls.

5. More than one glacier flowed through Yosemite Valley. The last covered just the lower valley walls and reached only as far as El Capitan and Bridalveil Fall.

the ocean plate and the continental plate changed from subduction to translation, in which the ocean floor no longer dives under the continent. Instead, both plates now move westward, but with the ocean plate also still moving northward relative to the continental plate. Such a condition is not stable, and is responsible for many California earthquakes; the boundary between the plates is the highly active San Andreas fault. Also at this time (about 15 to 25 million years ago), the Sierra Nevada began its current rise.

A Mountain Range is Formed

While the prior volcanic mountain range was being removed by erosion, the region's surface became one of gentler relief with slower-moving streams. Deep soil formed. Just south of Yosemite the San Joaquin River drained across the Sierra from headwaters east of the present range crest.

Then uplift of the range quickened. (This uplift continues today.) Lavas flowed again, now on a new surface, mainly in the northern range, but as far south as Yosemite's Tuolumne River drainage. Flows erupted into valleys and buried their stream channels, preserving their courses as though fossils of a bygone landscape. Also buried

3. Continuing uplift caused the Merced to erode an intricate, steep-walled canyon. Into this, tributary streams cascaded from the original upland plateau.

6. After the ice melted, a lake formed. This Lake Yosemite flooded the entire valley. The Merced River slowly filled the ancient lake with silt and sand until it eventually became the level valley floor we see today.

n the channels was the gold that the stream gravels contained, washed in from deposits up-slope; the lavas concealed the yellow metal for eons, until a species—humans—was to come along to discover and cherish it.

About 5 to 10 million years ago, the touching plates produced tension in the earth's crust. The crust stretched so much that it cracked into large blocks, one of which became the Sierra Nevada. That block broke on the east, where the range fronts Nevada, and tilted downward to the west under the Great Valley of California.

During this uplift erosion accelerated, pro-ducing a new landscape of steeper slopes within the more undulating older contours. Remnants of the older surface persist, although complicated by the various weathering patterns on the differ-ent rocks composing them. One such erosion sur-face is evident on the slopes of peaks near Tioga Pass on the eastern boundary of the park—peaks such as Shepherd Crest, North Peak, and the north shoulder of Mount Dana. Another is the upland surface at the rim of Yosemite Valley, on which Sentinel Dome and North Dome stand. Carved within these surfaces are the canyons of the Merced and Tuolumne rivers; their original V-shaped profiles still exist in the unglaciated canyons downstream from Yosemite and Hetch Hetchy valleys, such as the Merced Canyon below El Portal.

THE ADVANCE OF THE ICE

As the range was being uplifted toward its present height, the climate of the entire earth began to cool. This was some three million years ago; the Ice Age was beginning. Glaciers began to form in the High Sierra. As they grew and descended through stream canyons, they exerted a powerful force, polishing the rocks that were hard and massive and quarrying the rocks that were fissured. They cut away the lower walls of the valleys and transformed them into U-shapes, emphasizing with bolder strokes the landshaping that the streams had already begun.

The question of just how many glaciers descended through Yosemite Valley cannot be answered satisfactorily today. A large glacier nearly always erodes away the evidences of ear-lier, smaller glaciers. There may have been many more waxings and wanings of ice streams than we know about, and the story may very well be much more complex than geologists have so far been able to determine, or perhaps ever can.

The largest glacier (we call this the "largest" glacier, although this series may have had two or more that were just as extensive) filled Yosemite Valley completely, overtopping North Dome and Glacier Point and extending down-canyon to El Portal ten miles beyond Yosemite Valley and 2,000 feet lower. In the glacial episode or episodes that occurred during and perhaps prior to this largest glacier, most of the soil that had formed on the Sierra during the long period of weather-ing that preceded the Ice Age was scraped away.

The bedrock floor of Yosemite Valley was also gouged, and a trough was created; it was as deep as 2,000 feet below the present ground sur-face and 6,000 feet below the then-maximum ice surface. A bedrock lip remained at the west end

Majestic Nevada Fall leaps grandly to a lower level, descending in the bed of the glacier that once moved from the High Sierra to Yosemite Valley. The fall's massive granite cliff was too resistant for the ice to quarry. Liberty Cap—a dome once overridden by ice— stands beyond, a glacial monument giving us a scale by which to envision how thick the ice was.

of this valley trough, and all the debris that eroded from the valley floor had to be lifted by the ice over this barrier. This was not an impossible task, since the slowly flowing ice was more than a mile deep in the upper valley. It also had behind it the force supplied from its nourishing, ice-producing tributaries upstream—strength that allowed the glacier to carry up and over such an obstacle not only sand and boulders, but even the large blocks that were impacted into its lower-most layers.

The last glacier, or series of glaciers, of which we have a record in Yosemite Valley was not nearly as large. It polished the lower valley walls and left terminal moraine ridges in the lower end of the valley, arcing between El Capitan and Bridalveil Fall. Behind these natural dams, in the depression scoured by this latest glacier in the valley deposits, a lake formed (as others probably had following earlier glaciations). This lake was almost seven miles long; geologists refer to this ancient landmark as "Lake Yosemite." The rivers of water that had now taken the place of the ice streams filled the lake with silt and sand, and rock fell into the lake from canyon walls. Finally the lake—and the magnificent images that it

Bridalveil Fall drops from its hanging valley into the Yosemite chasm—one of several spectacular sidestreams that do the same and thus help produce the grandest collection of waterfalls in all the world. The fall's cliff was largely cut away by the Yosemite Valley glaciers. At one time ice here was thick: it extended above the highest of the three Cathedral Rocks, standing above and left of the waterfall.

undoubtedly reflected—vanished. In the area where it had lain, sedges and willows became established. Then, as other plants and trees gradually moved onto favorable valley sites, the broad meadow-and-forest floor we know today as Yosemite Valley began to develop.

Before the glaciers came, the side streams of Yosemite, Bridalveil, Ribbon, Sentinel, and Illilouette creeks had dropped into the valley as cascades; unlike the larger and more powerful Merced River, they had not been able to downcut their courses as rapidly. The same conditions existed when the glaciers passed through, and the glaciers in the main valley eroded their pathways more rapidly than those in the side valleys eroded theirs.

As the main-valley glaciers widened the gorge, they cut off the lower channels of the tributary valleys, leaving them steeper yet and with their upper portions "hanging" even more. Subsequently, the cliffs thus produced have been undermined and steepened further due to wetting of their lower portions by spray from the plunging streams. This wetting of the waterfall bases, coupled with repeated freezing and thawing, has promoted more rapid "spalling" or removal of bedrock there than higher on the cliffs. These streams that now drop into Yosemite Valley constitute some of the highest waterfalls in the world. Waterfalls on the main river, such as Vernal Fall and Nevada Fall, however, merely drop over steps cut where there were soft or fractured rock masses that the ice could erode effectively.

DOMES AND JOINTING

The earlier glaciers overrode some of the domes, such as those on the north side of the valley—North Dome, Basket Dome, and Mount Watkins—but did not completely cover those to the south—Half Dome, Sentinel Dome, and Mount Starr King. The upper slopes of Half Dome, for example, are estimated to be 3 to 10 million years old; since they were shaped long before the main Ice Age, they cannot be the work of the glaciers. Even if the Yosemite examples were not convincing evidence that glaciers did not shape all the domes, there is certainly proof in the domes of Stone Mountain, in Georgia, and those of Rio de Janeiro, in Brazil, none of which ever knew the raspy touch of a glacier. It is *exfoliation*, not glaciation, that forms domes.

What is exfoliation? It is the process in which rock shells are cast off as the rock expands. Exfo-liation is usually the result of heat, freezing, or the absorption of moisture, but these localized effects can hardly account for the scale on which exfoliation occurs on Yosemite's massive domes and cliffs. For example, the rock layers on the Royal Arches are as thick as two hundred feet in places, and some exfoliation plates extend for hundreds of yards.

At Yosemite exfoliation by load relief has been the dominant landshaping process. The rocks here were once buried perhaps as much as five miles below the surface of the earth. Once at the surface, these rocks expand, since they are no longer subjected to the pressure under which they were formed. Slowly, cracks form parallel to exposed surfaces, creating layers that break up and fall off more slowly still, leaving few sharp angles. Exfoliation is especially prominent in Yosemite because of the many occurrences here of

Half Dome (on the right) appears in a less familiar view. Down Tenaya Canyon, in the middle ground, once flowed one of the major ice streams that entered Yosemite Valley (beyond to the right). This Tenaya Canyon glacier reached halfway up the cliff face of Half Dome, burying most of the land in this view. Stark granite has formed little soil since that time of glaciers and supports few trees.

massive, unfissured granite. Rock in other areas is more closely fractured; it falls apart in pieces and thus shells cannot develop, nor can domes and massive cliffs.

None of Yosemite's domes is perfectly round; all deviate in shape somewhat, and a few even seem to have split, the result of the influence of *joints* (comparable to master cracks in a masonry wall), one of the most important elements that have shaped the land in Yosemite. Joints may be tiny cracks or just planes along which pressure or friction has weakened the rock crystals or their bonds, allowing fluids to pass more easily. Joints in otherwise massive rock provide avenues for more rapid erosion, as in The Fissures at Taft Point where only local snowmelt or raindrops trickle into the cracks, yet the effect is deep, open gashes in the otherwise unjointed rock.

Horizontal joints on the Yosemite Falls cliffs, some of which are marked by brushy ledges, occur at the bottom of the Upper Fall and at the top of the Lower Fall. The Three Brothers, symmetrical rock spires on the north side of Yosemite

...al Arches took shape as exfoliation (casting off "rock ...ves") caused its massive lower portions to fall away. ...th Dome, towering above, illustrates the rounding ...uence that exfoliation can exert in the landshaping ...cess. Washington Column stands on the right.

Valley, were formed as the result of intersecting sets of parallel joints, the most prominent set of which slopes about 45 degrees downward to the west. And of course there is the face of Half Dome, Yosemite's most famous landmark, where joints follow the same vertical, northeast-southwest trend that is the principal joint pattern in Yosemite. This same trend is also found in the Nevada Fall cliff and the adjacent canyons of Liberty Cap, Mount Broderick, and the back of Half Dome. Tenaya Canyon and many canyons and streams located north of the Tuolumne River, as well as zigzagging portions of Yosemite Valley itself, also follow the regional trend, along vertical joints both exposed and concealed.

Just as joints can control the topography, so can the *absence* of joints. El Capitan is the best example. Only discontinuous cracks flaw the bold faces of this monolith, which stands at the narrowest part of the valley, opposite the almost-as-massive Cathedral Rocks. Neither formation has any significant talus pile (rock rubble) at its base, and both are made up largely of the same strong El Capitan granite, from a band that apparently once crossed the valley here. However, just down the valley are the Rockslides, an immense pile of talus that developed below highly fractured diorite, rock that does not have nearly the strength of some of Yosemite's other granitic rocks.

Symmetry of angled slopes and upright faces at the Three Brothers was caused by master joint cracks, as was most of Yosemite Valley's scenery patterns. Glaciers sculptured as the joints allowed.

At the opposite end of the valley from the Rockslides and El Capitan stands a series of domes: North Dome, Basket Dome, Mount Watkins, Half Dome, Mount Broderick, Liberty Cap, Sentinel Dome, and the Starr King group. All are composed of the same type of rock—Half Dome granodiorite —except for Sentinel Dome, which is composed of El Capitan granite. These two rock types (named after their most prominent examples) constitute virtually all of the outstanding rock formations that are present in Yosemite Valley.

THE LANDSCAPE TODAY

Thus we find that, as profound as were the effects of streams and glaciers in the formation of Yosemite Valley, they were not the most signifi-

cant of the forces that produced the masterpiece that is Yosemite. After all, these forces were widespread all over the earth, yet there is only *one* Yosemite. Geologists think that the aspect and appearance of the awesome Yosemite Valley is due to factors that are inherent in the locality. These factors are: (1) the internal character of the rocks found here—their chemistry, mineralogy, texture, and grain size—and (2) the way they fractured in response to forces exerted upon them. Streams and glaciers could not erode the rocks that were too strong to fracture; these resistant rocks were left as massive outcroppings that have exfoliated into the sheer cliffs and rounded domes that we see today. The weaker rocks that once surrounded these features have succumbed to erosion; thus the formations that are left now stand out in solitary splendor.

Landshaping is a process that never ends. In the time since the Ice Age glaciers melted away, rockslides have fallen, waterfalls have eroded their bases to drop more steeply, the last Lake Yosemite has been filled, and the Merced River meanders where that ancient lake once shimmered. And so nature's work goes on. Just as Yosemite does not now appear as it once did, so will it be different in the future. We are seeing it at only one moment in time. Perhaps someday all this will be no more; or perhaps nature's agents will have created a landscape that is more beautiful still (if we can imagine such a thing). We can only enjoy and cherish Yosemite as it is today, at the same time marveling at nature's ability to create and destroy and create again. Wonder is the special province of humans, and there is no better place to renew this precious quality than at Yosemite, a gift of creation.

SUGGESTED READING

BATEMAN, PAUL C., and CLYDE WAHRHAFTIG. "Geology of the Sierra Nevada." *Geology of Northern California,* Geol. Bul. 190. San Francisco: Calif. Div. of Mines, 1966.

HILL, MARY. *Geology of the Sierra Nevada.* Berkeley: Univ. of Calif., 1975.

HUBER, N. KING. "The Geologic Story of Yosemite National Park." U.S. Geological Survey Bulletin 1595. Washington, D.C.: Superintendent of Documents, 1987.

JONES, WILLIAM R. *Domes, Cliffs, and Waterfalls: A Brief Geology of Yosemite Valley.* Yosemite National Park: Yosemite Natural History Assn., 1976.

MATTHES, FRANCOIS E. *The Incomparable Valley: A Geologic Interpretation of the Yosemite.* Berkeley: Univ. of Calif., 1956.

The massive form of El Capitan (meaning "The Chief" among the tallest unbroken cliffs in all the world, stand shrouded above the Merced Rive

JEFF GNASS

The High Sierra

Contrast marks the High Sierra in Yosemite National Park. Rock, water, and sky come together in bold edges where lakes lap against granite shores, rock spires penetrate billowy thunderheads, and streams flash in the sun like slivers of crystal. There is a stark rawness here that all of life seems to sense: Deer pause at meadow borders; trees assume bonsai forms in lines along joint cracks; and pikas call in squeaky tones from under jagged boulder piles.

The landscape *looks* like what it *is*— a land that has just been created. Its sculptors—the glaciers—have gone, of course, and have been gone for at least 10,000 years, but their trails shine on in this fresh and exhilarating atmosphere.

In the "high country" the processes of nature seem to compete for dominance more than they do in the hospitable land below. Avalanches command the steeper slopes in winter, ripping through forests that will long show the slide paths as treeless corridors. Rocks roll into lakes and then, when the water freezes and expands, are pushed back out, forming shoreline ramparts. Frost action churns the soil that plants would otherwise stabilize with their roots.

The barrenness left by the glaciers is softened only where debris has lodged in basins or on shallow slopes, allowing life-filled meadows and forests to develop. But elsewhere the terrain is much as it was when the glaciers melted away—strewn with erratics (boulders dropped by the glaciers) on polished rock pavements, lined with moraine ridges at the edges of former glacier channels, dotted with deep-blue lakes perched on granite benches among the domes, and laced by streams that cascade here and there over bedrock slopes.

High on the shaded ridges of Mount Lyell the glacier trails are the freshest of all. In fact, we can see living glaciers there now. These glaciers

DAVID MUENCH

A high-country dwarfed lodgepole pine—as old as some of its much-taller counterparts in the forests—finds sustenance in the harsh soil of a granite niche. It is a plant pioneer in the High Sierra.

Yosemite's living Lyell Glacier is evidence that the Ice Age may not have entirely passed. From Mount Lyell standing above the ice at the highest point in the park ice once moved downslope in several directions Glaciers covered most of the park's High Sierra and spilled into the Hetch Hetchy and Yosemite valleys

Hetch Hetchy Valley lies north of Yosemite Valley in the western part of Yosemite National Park. At one time Hetch Hetchy was a near-rival in natural beauty to its famed sister Yosemite Valley (both have waterfalls and domes and similar geologic origins), but a dammed reservoir now floods Hetch Hetchy's former meadows and groves. John Muir and other conservationists fought to keep Hetch Hetchy pristine, and the story makes a chapter in American conservation literature, for national parks and dams rarely mix.

are not merely remnants of the past; they are new, having formed and reformed within the last two or three thousand years, a period of time that coincides with man's recorded history. While looking at the reality of these living glaciers, the question of whether the Ice Age is over may seem absurd.

A WORLD OF ICE AND SNOW

Standing on Yosemite's highest point atop Mount Lyell, above the Lyell Glacier and gazing down the Lyell Fork of the Tuolumne River, it is easy to envision, in imagination, the longest ancient glacier of the Sierra Nevada as it once crawled along its sixty-mile trail: We can "see" ice extending away in all directions from this point.

The summit itself is bare rock. Howling winds blow falling snow over the peak into the great canyon heads all around us, where the once-light flakes pile so deeply that their accumulated weight on the bottom layers causes the snow to crystallize into ice and move away from the overburdening pressure, flowing down the slopes under gravity.

Cathedral Peak in the Tuolumne Meadows region of the High Sierra stands above meadow grasses, sedges, and wildflowers of lower Cathedral Lake's shallows. A distinctive type of granite rock, named for this peak and occurring in its vicinity, is also found as isolated "erratic" boulders in distant Yosemite Valley, transported there by glaciers.

During the Ice Age one such ice stream flowed from the north slopes of the mountain clear to Hetch Hetchy Valley, at Tuolumne Meadows spilling a major lobe that flowed down Tenaya Canyon into Yosemite Valley. Another started from the south side of Mount Lyell and eventually joined the lobe at Yosemite Valley, but it reached there by way of Nevada Fall and Vernal Fall. A third glacier flowed east from this same summit, scouring its headwall back as if to join the other two glaciers that were eating into the cirques on the other sides of the peak.

There was other action: Rocks fell from the summit ridges out onto the ice; crevasses opened and closed; ice-blocks (seracs) tumbled down icefalls as the glaciers crept downslope.

Only higher peaks stood above the ice. (A map of the park during the glacial age would have been mostly white.) Nearly all of the High Sierra was covered, the ice rounding and polishing the rock surfaces as it moved across them. Taking the "ice line" as the boundary between the smooth lower slopes and the steep, hackly upper ones on castellated summits such as Cathedral and Unicorn peaks, the glacier at Tuolumne Meadows was more than 2,000 feet thick!

DAVID MUENCH

Glacier erratics lie where they were abandoned by the ice that moved down Tenaya Canyon on its way to Half Dome and Yosemite Valley.

Tuolumne Meadows' Pothole Dome was scalloped by water flowing under the glacier that was once here. Elsewhere, flatter polished slabs are true glacial polish, showing where the ice itself smoothed the rock.

Overleaf: A frame of autumnal brilliance warms the starkness of Half Dome. Photo by David Muench.

FRANK S. BALTHIS

DAVID MUENCH

An inside view of a Yosemite glacier reveals a mix of rock and ice, a blend that cuts much more deeply than ice alone!

Lembert Dome and all the domes at Tuolumne Meadows were buried under the ice, as were Moraine Dome in Little Yosemite Valley and North Dome at the head of Yosemite Valley itself. The polished bedrock canyons at Merced Lake on the upper Merced River and Pywiack Cascade in Tenaya Canyon below Clouds Rest were then slippery glacier beds. The glacier lobe that branched into Yosemite Valley from Tuolumne Meadows flowed over a shallow divide, passed Fairview Dome, and descended over Medlicott, Pywiack, and Polly domes into a zone of fractured granite, quarrying out the blocks there to form the basin that would be Tenaya Lake. But of course all of this landscape—all of these domes—was not visible; all was below the ice, waiting for its place in the sun.

Glaciation of Yosemite's High Sierra was not just a one-time thing; a chronology of ice invasions that spanned millions of years occurred. But finally the climate changed and the land once again became warmer. The glaciers ran out of the snow and ice that had been supplied upstream, and they stagnated on their beds. Slowly, as they melted and vanished, their burdens of rock fragments were lowered to the ground and left in rubbly piles. Occasionally the glacier snouts readvanced slightly, pushing up ridges. Meltwater from the dwindling volumes of the ice coursed about among the blocks of ice and heaps of debris, washing away the finer material and reworking the gravels, leaving the large boulders where they lay—where they *still* lie.

Geologically speaking, only a little time has passed since the ice melted, and the evidences of the power of the glaciers are still very much a part of the scene. But in the lower elevations, where the ice melted first, the glacier trails are not as obvious. Much of the softening probably occurred just after the glaciers died, as boulders tumbled into canyon bottoms and streams carried silt into the lakes. Living things could not, of course, gain a foothold until this loose debris achieved some stability.

Plants in a Changing Land

During the Ice Age, when the climate of much of the world was cooler, many alpine plants were forced to ever-lower elevations, as temperatures dropped and snowfall increased. Once beyond the influence of the cold, they spread laterally, colonizing the greater area available to them—such as the shores of lakes that had formed in the desert of the Great Basin. There they intermingled with other plants that had moved down the slopes of nearby mountains. Meanwhile, arctic plants moved southward, in front of the advancing continental glaciers, and mixed with the alpine plants.

When the glaciers melted and the climate warmed, some of the mountain plants migrated northward, establishing themselves in areas where they had never grown before. And many of the arctic plant species gradually migrated upward into the High Sierra where, together with local alpine plants, they became isolated on high peaks.

The locating and relocating of plants must have been repeated several times as warm climates and cold climates waxed and waned. Now some of the same species found along the Arctic Ocean also grow on isolated summits in Yosemite, even though these two regions are now separated by desert and forest habitats through which the plants cannot migrate. Some colonies probably vanished completely from lower summits as the warming climate pushed their necessary habitat conditions upward and right off the tops of these low peaks, taking along with them into oblivion any creatures that depended upon them for food or shelter.

DAVID MUENCH

Sun-bleached heartwood, wind-abraded bark, and a misshapen but oddly graceful stance of this ancient western juniper offer dramatic proof of the tree's ability to survive in the harsh environment of its rugged upper Tenaya Canyon home. Storms have pruned one side, leaving branches and leaves only where protected from prevailing winds.

Bands of pollen from fir and lodgepole pine trees plaster boulders at the edge of Tenaya Lake, marking stands of water as levels dropped from spring highs. In late summer, outlet streams from High Sierra lakes like this one often run dry. A clump of alpine laurel brightens the scene now, but ice and snow dominate most of the year.

27

GALEN ROWELL

High granite walls, richly coated by gleaming glacial polish, rise on the side of the Tuolumne River canyon. On the lower buttress, crescent-shaped "chattermarks" are impact cracks. Rocks embedded in the glacier that went by here snagged momentarily on the bedrock, causing the ice to advance in chattering steps.

As these alpine plants returned to the High Sierra, they aided in the formation of soil. Lichens loosened individual crystals from solid rock; trees pried cracks apart with their expanding roots; sedges and grasses caught silt along stream and lake edges and held it there to form turf that eventually became meadows and alpine rock gardens. Lodgepole pine from the forests below moved upward into high country, climbing higher with each succeeding generation.

In Yosemite treeline rose until it reached a height of 11,000 feet, where it remains today. There the whitebark pine continues its struggle, putting forth tentative shoots into the persistent wind. But the flying sand and ice that constantly assail these trees deform them into a "flag" shape,

all foliage remaining on the side away from the wind, until finally even the semi-protected leaves are abraded away. In the area just above treeline, the whitebarks grow as matted shrubs nestled in hollows among the rocks, and they do not survive at all at higher elevations.

Today the *bergschrund* crevasse at the head of Lyell Glacier is again nearly at the place where it was during the Ice Age. Once again, meltwater flows into the bergschrund, penetrating the cracks in the rocks below, freezing in the cold of the shadows and widening the cracks. As the resultant expansion splits and shears the rock, blocks lodge in the ice mass and begin the journey downslope. Now, however, they do not journey very far down the canyon; the boulders come up again at the toe of the ice only a half mile away, forming concentric moraine ridges.

Below the moraine milky streams tumble over rocky ledges to alpine meadows, where the turf is only beginning to swallow the glacial boulders. Smoothly fluted mounds of gray granite crop up from the green carpet of alpine grasses, flashing their polished planes in the Sierra sun. Thin scratches and deep grooves mar their billowy surfaces. These imperfections are the signatures of the glacier that scraped the outcrops with other rocks that were dragged along its bed, grinding both large and small fragments against each other and against bedrock to produce floury granules, the same substance that colors the milky water now flowing past. Here and there the repetition of semicircular cracks on the bedrock reveals a different kind of movement: rock chunks within the bottom ice of the glacier were pressed down so tightly against the bedrock by the tons of ice above that, instead of passing smoothly along, the glacier-encased chunks stalled from the friction before finally jumping ahead in chattering steps, upon impact permanently marking the bedrock. And an occasional metamorphic boulder, streaked or spotted reddish or dark-gray, perches atop a light granite outcropping well above the level of today's streams, carried there somehow from its parent bed high in the cirque walls of Mount Lyell.

The High Sierra has a *boreal* climate. Snow buries much of the upper range for more than

solar radiation in the thin atmosphere). Often, little or no rain falls from the end of May until October, so that once the snowmelt has run off, the crystalline soil drains and becomes as arid as desert sand. Torrents of water from sudden cloudbursts may wash soil from tree roots and deposit gravel strips over the meadow grasses. Lightning may shatter trees and set them afire, and driving hail may shear the blossoms from alpine flowers just when they are ready for pollination and seed production.

The sparse plants here respond in their own ways to such harsh conditions. Most of them—such as the white heather, alpine willow, mountain sorrel, and draba—grow close to the ground, often in little cushions, to escape the wind that prevails only a few inches above the ground. They also grow hairs on their stems and leaves, an adaptation that retards evaporation of the already scant moisture that is available to them. Flowering plants burst forth in showy blossoms that attract the few insects and birds that live here. Furthermore, the plants that grow here have become predominantly perennials; if they cannot reproduce one year, they will still have a chance to do so the next!

An angler tries for trout at one of the glacial lakes dotting the High Sierra. Many Yosemite lakes are naturally fishless, good for frogs.

JOSEF MUENCH

half the year, and in shaded areas of the highest regions it may not melt at all in summer. The very name of the range, the Spanish *Sierra Nevada* ("snowy mountain range"), reflects its character. Snow has been known to fall at a rate of five feet per day, and up to ten feet have accumulated in week-long storms. During such periods many trees are bent over by the weight of their snowy burdens, and some never straighten up again. Avalanches of snow race downslope, breaking trees and carrying them and other debris far out onto the meadows and frozen lakes.

Plants must do all their growing in the summer, a very short season at best. Near the glaciers the growing season is less than 60 days long and is full of uncertainties: A midsummer night may be freezing cold, even though the preceding day was uncomfortably hot (a result of the intense

The first animals that returned to the region after the glaciers melted were probably insects, traveling on the wind. Even today dragonflies are found on the glaciers, blown there from elevations far below. Other insects arrived along with their host plants. One such was the lodgepole-pine needleminer, a little moth whose larvae utilize the needles of that particular tree only. The needleminer drills into the foliage for food and shelter, then emerges every odd-numbered year to fly in swarms, reproduce, deposit more eggs, and die.

This situation is an example of a natural balance. Man need not take sides either to aid the insects in their fight for survival or to try to eliminate them in order to help save the trees. At times so many larvae are at work that they kill their too-generous hosts, and the result is the "ghost forests" of dead, bleaching trees that are present throughout much of the lodgepole range in the park. But the forest as a whole is not endangered. Needleminer outbreaks are spotty and last only a few years, until a cooler, rainy period occurs in which the moths fail to reproduce as effectively. Neither the needleminer nor the lodgepole pine seems likely to win the struggle; it merely continues as it has for so many thousands of years.

Together with the insects came, quite naturally, their predators, the birds. Mountain chickadees and flycatchers have a field day when the millions of needleminers hatch. The rosy finch, which took up residence on the permanent snowfields long ago, still flits about, eating hapless insects immobilized by the cold. The blue grouse is secure in its niche eating the food that is most abundant in this bird's area in winter as well as summer—needles from the fir trees. The Clark's nutcracker also lives on tree food, tearing white-bark pinecones apart to get at the nuts inside.

Many birds that come to the high country stay just for the summer, to mate and breed. The brightest of these is the crimson, yellow, and black male western tanager. Strangest to see here is the California gull, so far from the sea, although the white pelican once found on Lyell Glacier must have been an even odder sight.

Deer apparently arrived soon after their shrubby forage plants became established. Today the whole region is crisscrossed with their migration trails. In years when winter hits suddenly with an early-autumn snow, the deer literally run to the west and downhill, lest they be caught in

"Black" bears (usually brown here) may prowl any time of year in Yosemite's lower forests, denning only when food is scarce, snow deep, or when giving birth. Gone is the grizzly bear, namesake for Yosemite (from the Indian "uzumati").

the high country for the winter and suffer certain death. Bighorn sheep, reintroduced into the Yosemite region in 1986, graze the higher slopes above the deer's normal range, but winter on the east side of the Sierra. Mountain lions and coyotes came to prey on the deer; they remain today. Wolves may have been here, but if so, they have since disappeared from the region. Gone, too, are the grizzly bears that once roamed all of California. Black bears, however, are still common.

Most of the animals now living in the High Sierra seem to be too far south: the white-tailed jackrabbit, which turns white in winter; the weasel, which in winter becomes the ermine; the marmot and Belding ground squirrel (picketpin), which hibernate beneath the snow. The pine marten, badger, and cony are residents, as are the fisher and wolverine, although rare ones.

Any fish that before the Ice Age lived in Yosemite's High Sierra lakes were destroyed, along with their stream homes, by the grinding glaciers and the cold. After the ice melted, the water habitat that was left would have been suited to trout if not for the waterfalls that were too high for them to jump. In modern times, however, rainbow, cutthroat, golden, and eastern brook trout have been stocked for the sport of the

CHUCK PLACE

Arranged on the High Sierra Loop Trail a day's hike apart are backcountry tent camps providing meals and lodging to hikers and horse riders. Vogelsang High Sierra Camp, here, is typical of the camps' scenic mountain settings.

The marmot is an unusual mammal to new high country visitors. Feeding on meadow grasses, it dens under nearby rocks, often sunning atop the highest.

angler who must bring back tangible evidence of a successful fishing trip. But more than half the lakes in the park are protected places where watery denizens can live without being endangered by exotic species, places where we humans can watch and learn.

Humans are, in fact, little more than visitors in Yosemite's High Sierra. When the first major storm of autumn occurs, most of the park rangers follow the deer downslope. Yet the region exerts a strong appeal to many people, compelling them to return again and again. It has inspired fine literature—John Muir's *My First Summer in the Sierra,* for example—and excursions into its vastness served as one of the means by which the Sierra Club first rallied its members.

Every summer new enthusiasts discover the hundreds of miles of trails that crisscross the High Sierra, venturing forth to hike and backpack for the first time. More and more hikers are taking up cross-country rambles as they gain familiarity with the area. Some of the most hardy are even trying technical rock-climbing in their constant search for routes that will take them to places where few have been before or to places where the view has been reported to be especially inspiring.

Even today, at many places in Yosemite's wilderness, a hiker can spend an entire day without meeting another person. For a few, just the *sign* of one of their own species spoils the wilderness experience. For these purists, there is one last wilderness left—the white wilderness of the cold months with large areas where all signs of people are completely covered. Not many people are privileged to experience this pristine world; a lucky few slip quietly in on skis over the crystal snow and frozen lakes. Perhaps, for these few, even the solitude of nature in winter is not enough. Yearning also for the drama of action in their landscapes, perhaps they imagine—or even hope to *see*— a time when the glaciers once again travel the High Sierra trails.

SUGGESTED READING

BOWEN, EZRA. *The High Sierra.* New York City: Time-Life Books, 1972.

MUIR, JOHN. *My First Summer in the Sierra.* Boston: Houghton Mifflin, 1911.

O'NEILL, ELIZABETH STONE. *Meadow in the Sky: A History of Yosemite's Tuolumne Meadows Region.* Fresno, Calif.: Panorama West Books, 1983.

The Giant Sequoia

The giant sequoia is not only the largest living thing on the face of the earth, it also has the distinction of having achieved a life span that stretches into thousands of years. The formula by which the giant sequoia has reached such great size and age is simple: It grows as long as it lives (as do all trees), and it lives for a long, long time. Thus this great giant can truly be said to represent "life at maximum."

Most species, even those that live inordinately long lives, do not persist for long before some change in their environment forces them to take on new characteristics or even develop into a different form! Many fail to adapt; these species die out and eventually become extinct, perhaps leaving only a few fossils as evidence of their existence. The giant sequoia, however, can be traced, through its own fossils and those of its relatives, as far back as 200 million years ago, to a time when its ancestors, existing in a very similar form, forested much of the earth.

Today, however, the giant sequoia is truly a relict species, occurring only in isolated groves on the western slope of California's Sierra Nevada, a location that apparently fulfills the climatic conditions that these trees require for growth and reproduction. Three of these groves are located within Yosemite National Park. (Sequoia and Kings Canyon National Parks contain thirty groves, and the remaining groves lie outside national park boundaries, mainly in areas administered by the U. S. Forest Service and the State of California.) Despite the limitations of its range, the giant sequoia is healthy and reproduces adequately. Some giant sequoias have been successfully propagated in sites nearby—but outside the tree's normal range—such as Wawona and Yosemite Valley. It also has been grown in Sacramento (California), Reno (Nevada), and even Europe.

"Of all living things," wrote one admirer, "only the giant sequoia is assured of living long enough to be struck by lightning." Thus it is that nearly every mature giant sequoia bears the scars of lightning-caused fires, some of which are very extensive. But even the most severe burn damage may not succeed in destroying this tree, with its incredible ability to survive against seemingly overwhelming odds.

Estimates of the age to which a giant sequoia may grow vary widely—up to an extreme of 10,000 years. But no giant sequoia that now exists has lived for longer than about 3,000 years. Only

This chickaree (Douglas squirrel) is dining while perched on a needled branch. In the giant sequoia forest, the chickaree unknowingly but efficiently aids in that tree's reproduction: The squirrel scatters countless seeds (too small for regular use as food) over the forest floor as it eats the tree's fleshy cones.

The Grizzly Giant in Yosemite's Mariposa Grove is one of the world's largest trees. Although not as old as some other "big trees," few others seem so ripe with age, perhaps because of its lightning-induced snag top and pronounced lean. Now removed, cables were once installed to keep the tree up! But with or without man, nature's way is for this 2,700-year-old veteran to fall someday.

the bristlecone pine is older; the age of a specimen in eastern Nevada has been estimated at about 4,600 years. Quite unlike the stately giant sequoia, these bizarrely twisted and stunted pines live at treeline, rarely attaining a height of over 50 feet.

The Largest Living Thing

It is the sheer bulk of the giant sequoia that gives it the edge over its competitors. Sizes of these trees are computed on the basis of trunk volume. The great girth and great height of the giant sequoia combine to provide more cubic feet than any other living organism in today's world.

Yosemite's Grizzly Giant, for instance, has a volume of more than 30,000 cubic feet. (And it is not the largest giant sequoia, a distinction that belongs to the General Sherman tree in Sequoia National Park.) The trunk diameter of the Grizzly Giant tapers from 29 feet near its base to 14 feet at a height of 96 feet above ground, the point at which its first large limb sprouts, a limb that itself is six feet in diameter and bigger around than most of the large trees that grow below that height.

The giant sequoia (*Sequoiadendron giganteum*) is not the *tallest* tree in the world; nor is it the *broadest*. The tule cypress grows thicker and the coast redwood grows taller. The coast redwood (*Sequoia sempervirens*), a relative of the giant sequoia, may reach heights of over 350 feet, whereas the giant sequoia seldom grows over 300 feet. (Once the giant sequoia has reached this height, its growth is all *outward*.) Aside from shape, there are other differences between the giant sequoia (sometimes called "Sierra redwood") and the coast redwood, the most obvious one being that the bark of the giant sequoia is cinnamon-colored, whereas the bark of the coast redwood is more grayish-red. (The coast redwood gets its name instead from the color of its heartwood, a much-sought-after building material.)

Growing in fog-rich western California, the coast redwood occupies an environment that is entirely different from that of the Sierra's giant sequoia, yet it may seem strange that the two principal remnants of a family of trees that once were widespread throughout the world have retreated to grow only on opposite sides of California's Great Valley, one tree being the largest living thing and the other the tallest.

Surviving Against the Odds

The Grizzly Giant has been standing for 2,700 years and once was much taller. It made a great lightning target, however. In one storm alone it was hit six times; during the long years of its existence it, of course, must have seen many thousands of storms. Now it is but 209 feet tall. The first photograph of this tree, taken more than a century ago, showed it leaning at 17 degrees, and there has been concern ever since that it might fall. But today it still leans at the same angle, its bulk somehow balanced on its widely spreading but shallow root pad.

The Grizzly Giant will not die except through an "act of God," for its species has developed adaptations that make it highly resistant to most of its attackers, including insects and fungi. Perhaps, as did the road-spanning Wawona Tunnel tree in 1969, it will fall during a record snowfall, when the crushing weight of snow overloads its branches and causes an imbalance. Perhaps no one will be around to see the tree fall or even hear

FRANK S. BALTHIS

This rustic cabin—the Mariposa Grove Museum—gives scale to tall giant sequoias, helping explain man's admiration for the immense trees and his motivation to preserve them. In fact, a concern for trees is what led to creation of some of the first national parks, including Yosemite. The sequoia cone still adorns some leather and gold parts of the park ranger's uniform.

Most park visitors see the sequoia groves in summer, yet the trees live over half their lives with snow. Here in the Tuolumne Grove, a moderate snowfall droops branches of giant sequoia and companion trees. Larger Sierran snowfalls of several feet cause limbs—and occasionally even the trees themselves—to crash to earth. Few humans are present to witness such events.

its crash, for the heavy snow and high-wind conditions that could topple it might preclude the presence of any humans in the area.

Or perhaps a particularly violent lightning bolt will shatter its trunk or burn its life-supporting cambium layers to the point that it can no longer survive. Or the soil around its root base may become so water-saturated and mushy on the leaning side that it can no longer support the huge tree in its more-or-less upright position.

This giant has persisted throughout many similar stresses it has undoubtedly incurred in its vast lifetime. And, because it stands protected within a national park, it has little to fear from its only true enemy—humans. Thus nature alone will likely cause its death. Such a death is not something one likes to contemplate, but it is a thrill to imagine the earth-shaking, reverberating boom that this giant will make as, reacting to some incredibly severe strain, its two million pounds crash to earth—a venerable, noble giant at last relinquishing its tenacious hold on life!

THE GROVES

Of Yosemite's three giant-sequoia groves, the largest lies south of Yosemite Valley. Known as the Mariposa Grove, it contains the Grizzly Giant and is the best known and most visited.

Two smaller groves lie north of Yosemite Valley: The Tuolumne Grove contains a tree that

CHUCK PLACE

major river canyons, at elevations from 5,200 feet in the lower Merced Grove to 6,800 feet in the upper Mariposa Grove. Their climates vary from warm, dry summers to sunny winters interrupted by infrequent snowstorms that may last a day or a week, leaving several feet of new snow—or just a trace. High winds are not frequent where sequoias grow, but thunderstorms with lightning bolts are.

Why these trees are confined to isolated groves is a mystery, for there is much more area with the same environment available. Yet not even single trees are found naturally outside the boundaries of the groves. It's as if these giants have chosen to be friendly and live within the companionable proximity of others like themselves—if whimsy can be permitted—just like people do.

FIRE: FOE OR FRIEND?

Summer and autumn fires are also a part of the natural environment in which the giant sequoia lives. In fact, the mature sugar and yellow pines that live together with the giant sequoia in the mixed-conifer forests of the Sierra Nevada all rely on these occasional fires for their existence. Without fire to clear out the limb canopy overhead, the sunlight would not penetrate to the offspring of these sun-loving trees, and their seedlings would languish in the shadows below. The forests would fill instead with the shade-tolerant white fir and incense-cedar.

Forest managers have long known that fire is requisite to certain kinds of plant life; however, it is only in recent years that this natural law has begun to be understood by the public. Virtually all of the specimen trees in the groves show fire scars on their trunks, proving that they have survived many fires of the past. (Studies of annual rings show that the Mariposa Grove has burned, on the average, every 20 or 25 years.) Dry sequoia heartwood burns well, but the highly insulative characteristics of the mature tree's bark—which may be as thick as 18 inches—serve to retard fire.

Although fires have certainly caused great injury to some giant sequoia trees, burning them through and even killing some, fires have also

one can drive through—a standing stump that is called the Dead Giant. The Merced Grove is accessible only to hikers. In either of these smaller groves it is possible to find solitude under the ancient columns. Perhaps one can be alone for an entire day, a day well spent in reflection and contemplation. This is the same area where the giant sequoia was discovered by the Joseph Rutherford Walker trapping party who, on their way west in 1833, passed through the area that is now Yosemite National Park.

Like all sequoia groves, Yosemite's three stand on the slopes of upland ridges between created some spectacular, still-living shells—a source of constant amazement for curious people. They come to marvel at oddities such as the Corridor Tree, the Telescope Tree (in which you can stand inside and see the sky through the top), and the Clothespin Tree.

The "specimen" trees are the most dramatic features of the giant-sequoia groves; even so, one can easily become engrossed in studying other aspects of this wonderful tree—its life cycle, for example. The young seedlings, delicate and lacy-wreathed, look as if they are hardly capable of growing to the monstrous sizes that their adult relatives have attained.

Reproduction and Growth

The maturity of a giant sequoia is not necessarily indicated by huge size. The tree begins to produce seeds after only a few years of life. Mature trees generate about 600 *new* cones every year, each cone containing a few hundred healthy seeds, so that they produce more than 100,000 seeds annually. The *average* mature sequoia holds 10,000 cones in its branches, with perhaps two million seeds inside; and a *large* sequoia may bear as many as 40,000 cones.

But the cones do not just fall off the trees and release the seeds. This is done by an unknowing agent—the chickaree, or Douglas squirrel. This little tree squirrel relishes the fleshy scales of the sequoia cones, and as it feasts on them, the seeds, ignored by the busy diner, scatter on the forest floor. The chickaree is amazingly efficient in releasing the seeds of the giant sequoia. A single animal has been known to cut cones at a rate of more than 500 in half an hour, and more than 10,000 in a single season! Another agent is an insect borer—a beetle—that lives in the tree and severs dried cones from it.

Once the seeds reach the forest floor, they must overcome other problems before reproduction can take place. If the seeds come to rest on a thick duff of needles and twigs, reproduction fails. Sunlight and nourishment, in the forms of moisture and the minerals of bare soil, must be present. Fire, by clearing the forest floor, encourages such conditions. (That sequoia seedlings need access to bare mineral soil is evidenced by the fact that in those places in the groves where the soil has been turned up during road and building construction there is a solid screen of young sequoias, even though few seedlings are seen in other places nearby.)

Of course, in a fire the seeds that already lie on the ground are burned up, too. So nature

K.C. DEN DOOVEN

Fire gave the Mariposa Grove's Clothespin Tree its open trunk, enhancing this giant sequoia's appeal to park visitors.

provides yet another way to ensure reproduction of the giant sequoia: Heat rises in the branches and dries the cones. In a day or so, after the fire has died out, the cones open and release their seeds, which fall on the cooling ashes below. In a few months tiny sequoia seedlings protrude from the bare soil, vying for the honor of a place beside their giant parents. Most of the seedlings will die, of course, but because the giant sequoia has such a long life span, even if only *one* offspring of a mature giant sequoia is successful during the parent tree's lifetime, the population count of this tree will remain constant!

Fire is a force of nature: For millennia, light fires—caused by lightning strikes or purposely set—ran through Yosemite's forests, leaving the mature, bark-protected trees intact. But with establishment of the park, all fires were suppressed (to "protect" the trees). In the following century plus, underbrush and fallen logs collected. These became fuel for wildfires that, burning hotter, consumed the trees. Today, park and forest managers use prescribed burning to simulate nature's way; most naturally started fires at higher elevations are even allowed to burn their course.

New Concepts of Conservation

Because of the new understanding of the role that fire plays in the reproduction of the giant sequoia and other trees, park managers and conservationists have swung away from strict attempts to eliminate all fires. In some areas where the no-burn policy was in force for many years and thus inadvertently limited reproduction of the tree, "prescribed" fires in the groves and surrounding mixed-conifer forests have been set by park managers in an attempt to return the forests to the natural conditions that existed a century ago, a time when light, natural fires ran through the forests, burning the accumulated fallen limbs and pine needles so that no great build-up of fuel could occur.

Egg-shaped cones from sequoia trees litter the forest floor. Each carries the potential to start hundreds of new giants.

After so many years in which a policy of excluding *all* fire from the forests was followed, fire cannot today be allowed to run unchecked. The fuels that accumulated over the intervening century could easily feed an uncontrollable holocaust wherein fire, leaping swiftly across tree crowns, could devastate an entire forest, as it did in late summer and early fall of 1987. Certainly this is not nature's way in the Sierran forests, either.

With careful management we can only hope that the natural balance will be restored. In time, perhaps the sight of fire burning in a forest will not be thought of as something ugly and foreign, but as a natural and perhaps even beautiful part of nature.

John Muir, who was ahead of his time in many ways, was one who apparently looked upon fire as a harmonious part of the natural world. A century ago he described its "varied beauty" as he watched it move through a giant sequoia forest:

> *Fire grazing, nibbling on the floor...spinning thousands of little jets—lamps of pure flame... old prostrate trunks glowing like red-hot bars... Smoke and showers of white, fluffy ashes from the fire boring out trunks, rills of violet fire running up the furrows swiftly, lighting huge torches flaming overhead two hundred feet...black and lurid smoke surges steaming through the trees, the columns of which look like masts of ships obscured in scud and flying clouds.*

Such is the giant sequoia's environment, one that humans have been slow to understand, for it seems alien to our concept of an ideal habitat. Could it be that fire is neither friend nor foe, as the human mind might categorize it? Perhaps fire is just another of the numerous elements of the environment that this ancient giant species has learned to live with—and even utilize—in its millennia-spanning struggle for survival.

This thought introduces other questions: Could it be that the tree has been forced to retreat at other times in its history, times when the climate of the earth was as cool and moist as it is now? If the earth should enter into a period of drier climate, with more widespread fires, might not the giant sequoia regain its former range? Is it possible that the longevity of the giant sequoia and its giantism could serve to eliminate its vulnerability to the short climatic swings that seem to affect the human species so profoundly? Perhaps that is the purpose and value of these characteristics that to us are so marvelous.

LARRY ULRICH

Stately giant sequoias stand in the Mariposa Grove, showing the continuing vitality of the species—so long as ecologically sound choices are made for its future.

SUGGESTED READING

ENGBECK, JOSEPH H., JR. *The Enduring Giants*. Berkeley: Univ. of Calif., 1973.

HARVEY, H. T., H. S. SHELLHAMMER, R. E. STECKER, and R. J. HARTESVELDT. *Giant Sequoias*. Sequoia National Park: Sequoia Natural History Assn., 1980.

MUIR, JOHN. *Coniferous Forests and Big Trees of the Sierra Nevada*. Reprint. Golden, Colo.: Outbooks, 1980.

TWEED, WILLIAM C. *Sequoia-Kings Canyon: The Story Behind the Scenery*. Las Vegas, Nevada: KC Publications, 1980.

Man at Yosemite

Time is the most definite constant faced by man; yet it is the most elusive for him to grasp. Yosemite is located on an earth that is more than four billion years old and contains granites that are hundreds of millions of years old. Even its later glacial period covered hundreds of thousands of years.

Modern time—the time since the glaciers melted—is brief enough to measure in the only unit that is truly comprehensible to man—his own lifetime. Only a few hundred lifetimes have elapsed since the last extensive glaciers melted away.

During the time of the Ice Age, people made their way into North America across the Bering Strait, which was then an open land bridge, and dispersed into their new continent as generations passed. Some of the descendants might have seen Yosemite Valley when it was a lake and the area of Tenaya Lake when it was a glacier bed. The expanding human population settled in habitable niches wherever such places could be found, including those areas newly released from the icy grip of the glaciers.

Over the ensuing centuries, Yosemite's scenery was largely static. The waterfalls began to drop a little more steeply as their bases eroded into the walls. The glacial moraines lost their sharp ridge crests, and their angular boulders became more rounded. Some lakes filled in and became meadows. But most geologic activity was so minor and occurred so slowly that it probably was unnoticed by the peoples who populated the area.

Only recently have we begun to learn more of the lives, work, and dreams of these first peoples, although they lived in Yosemite more than forty times as long as have modern people. The few traces they left include arrowheads found scattered throughout the park, some bowl-shaped holes in flat-topped boulders where they ground acorns into flour, and a few weathered rock markings.

From remains at Crane Flat and El Portal we know that humans inhabited the area that is now the park at least 4,000 years ago (a period that covers more than the life span of the Grizzly Giant). All the evidence tells us that during this time these Indians lived close to nature, harvesting some of its bounty to meet their own needs.

K.C. DEN DOOVEN

Ancient residents of the Yosemite region ground acorns into flour on flat granite boulders, wearing deep mortar holes. Their legends explained the valley's formation and their fires kept the meadows clear.

Upper Yosemite Fall shines brightly as its column drop seemingly from the sky. Such valley scenes becam an inspiration for the park movement. The park ide began as early as the 1860s, partly in response to th strife then of Civil War. President Abraham Lincol signed the first Yosemite legislatior

Yosemite Valley's chapel dates from 1879 and is a symbol of the long history of valley settlement as well as the community spirit of pioneer residents. This winter view is a reminder that in early years access to the remote valley was difficult and few wintered here; the first who did so were teared lost long before spring came. Today, however, winter hardships are few compared to the chance to view valley scenes when draped in white.

The relationship between the Indian and nature was, in fact, the inspiration that led to the first proposal for a national park, made almost forty years before the idea was realized. Indian painter and explorer George Catlin, in an 1833 New York newspaper, proposed:

> *A nation's park, containing man and beast, in all the wild and freshness of their nature's beauty... where the world could see for ages to come, the native Indian in his classic attire, galloping his wild horse...amid the fleeting herds of elks and buffaloes.*

Strangely, Catlin's vision was made public the same year that other non-Indian people first entered the area that is now Yosemite National Park. Traveling west along the Mono Trail of the Indians, now the Tioga Road, Joseph Walker and his party of trappers "discovered" the Yosemite Valley (although they apparently did not actually enter the valley), the giant sequoias, and the High Sierra. In spite of all the grandeur that was unfolding before them, these men were disappointed. They were, after all, trappers, and their objective was to find beaver for pelts to sell to eastern United States and European fur hat markets. Because that animal is thought to have then been alien to this part of the mountains, the trappers likely did not find any until they reached the Central Valley west of the Sierra.

GOLD FEVER AND STRIFE

The Walker party had been observed by the Indians, but this intrusion did not disturb the natives greatly. In fact, in Yosemite all remained much as before until 1848. Then an event occurred some 100 miles to the north that would soon have an effect not only on the Indians of the Yosemite area but on the entire region, nation, and even the world. The gold that had eroded eons before from the rocks of the central Sierra was discovered in a foothill stream.

Explorer Kit Carson soon traced the placer gold to its source and, in so doing, discovered the first lode gold mine, near Mariposa on John Fremont's estate west of Yosemite. Interest in this area and the entire Mother Lode foothills region picked up immediately, and prospectors swarmed into the area all the next year, becoming well-known in history as the "49ers".

The man who figured most pivotally in this chapter of Yosemite's history was a real frontiersman: James Savage had been a foothill trader before gold was discovered. His relations with the Indians had been good (he had married into five tribes). With the gold rush his business boomed; both Indian and white miners came to his stores to obtain supplies. Prices, however, were set high by such operators, who may have profited more by mining the miners than the miners did mining the mines.

The miners spread their operations over the foothills and established centers of population that boomed for a while and then dwindled when, later, the gold played out. A few miners lifted their eyes to gaze upon the magnificent peaks of the High Sierra. Some wrote down their impressions, but these observations went largely unnoticed in the prevailing feverish atmosphere. It was gold, not scenery, that was the issue of the day!

The Indians, witnessing the activity of the miners and noting the increase in their numbers, were beginning to be apprehensive. The miners and Indians also clashed directly over territory, property, and rights; many abuses naturally occurred as a new society moved into an already occupied area. If the miners continued to come in such numbers, there would be more people than the land could support and still more clashes. With the prospect of diminishing resources to fulfill their survival needs, the native people perceived a threat to their welfare—surely they would suffer.

There were no frontiers left for these Indians in 1849, and so they determined to try to drive the miners out of the Sierra by burning the trading outposts and killing the operators. The first attack was launched upon Savage's South Fork station on the Merced River not far below Yosemite Valley. The miners retaliated, deciding that the Indians instead must be driven from the mountains and confined to reservations in the San Joaquin Valley. Thus began the Mariposa Indian War.

Trader Savage became Major Savage, in charge of the Mariposa Battalion of volunteers. It didn't take him long to head for the home of the band that had raided his post on the Merced, and so it was Savage and his soldiers who became, in 1851, the first group of non-Indians to *enter* Yosemite Valley. The purpose, of course, was not discovery, nor could they spend much time to enjoy the scenery; they were here to capture Indians. But it was snowing; the river was high and cold and hard to ford, and they couldn't even find their quarry. "It's a hell of a place" was Savage's succinct comment about the glories of Yosemite.

In spite of the hardships, there was at least one man in the party who was enthusiastic about the area. In fact, Dr. Lafayette Bunnell, a physician, was *so* enthusiastic that, at the campfire on

DAVID MUENCH

The formidable bulk of Half Dome is mantled in snow as winter settles over Yosemite Valley following a fresh snowfall. The evergreens are "sugared" and a cloud of mist obscures the granite walls. At such times, from the sun-drenched upper slopes, snow avalanches boom into the canyon.

DAVID MUENCH

THE CAUSE FOR CONSERVATION

In spite of all the publicity about this new western paradise, no one thought at first about preserving its natural scenery so that it could be enjoyed by other generations down through the years. Perhaps it was Horace Greeley, editor of New York's *Tribune*, who was the first to espouse the cause of protection for Yosemite. In 1859, inspired by the giant sequoias of the Mariposa Grove, he wrote:

> *If the village of Mariposas, the county, or the State of California, does not immediately provide for the safety of these trees, I shall deeply deplore the infatuation and believe that these giants might have been more happily located.*

Still, nothing happened toward the preservation of this scenic area. Then, in 1862, an accident of nature occurred that was to awaken the entire world to the need for preservation of our natural areas. In that year more than 100 inches of rain fell on the Sierra Nevada within a three-month period, generating a disastrous flood that crippled the transportation system of the whole state and inundated the gold mines on John Fremont's rich Mariposa Grant just west of Yosemite, a factor contributing to its bankruptcy.

It so happened that at this time, Frederick Law Olmsted, who designed New York's Central Park, was "on strike," having disagreed over a matter of principle with the park's founders. Fremont's New York creditors were thus able to hire the out-of-work Olmsted to superintend their newly acquired mines in far-off California.

About then, a hoax took place that drew more attention to the area. This was the bogus auction in which the whole of Yosemite Valley was "raffled away" at a dollar a chance. Olmsted, arriving in September, 1863, rapidly sized up the situation and immediately got behind the drive for a park. Legislation soon cleared Congress,

the first night in the valley, he suggested that it be named for its Indian inhabitants—known to the soldiers by the name Yosemite—the very tribe they hoped to remove! (This is the origin of the name *Yosemite*, although the Indians called themselves the *Ahwahneechee* and their valley *Ahwahnee.)*

And so the valley became known to this society using a written language, yet for another four years no adequate description of the marvelous valley reached the outside world. When it did, the valley's fame spread rapidly. Writers, artists, and photographers came to visit the area and give to the world the creations of their minds and hearts that this wondrous place inspired.

And so the national park idea became firmly established. Today it is Yellowstone that is officially recognized as our first national park, having been created in 1872, but it is obvious to us now that the writers and park managers of the day clearly thought of Yosemite as the first.

That Yosemite was meant to be considered a *national* resource, even though it was at first state-controlled, is borne out in statements by Olmsted, who is considered to be the "father of landscape architecture," a profession that served as the foundation upon which the new art of park planning grew. After the law that established the Yosemite Grant had made its way through Congress, Olmsted wrote an 1865 report recommending how the grant should be managed and stressing its national importance: "It is the will of the *nation* that this scenery...shall be held solely for public purposes."

and Abraham Lincoln signed the "Yosemite Grant" into law on June 30, 1864, when the Civil War was still in progress. Few parks have had a shorter legislative history.

Olmsted became chairman of the first board of commissioners to manage the Yosemite Grant, having been appointed by the governor of California, under whose charge the new park had been placed. Olmsted immediately set to work to prepare a "master plan" for the area. In his plan he philosophized about how the Civil War may have been the significant event that alerted the American people to the need to care for and preserve areas of unusual beauty for public use:

> It was during one of the darkest hours, before Sherman had begun the march upon Atlanta or Grant his terrible movement through the Wilderness, when the paintings of Bierstadt and the photographs of Watkins, both productions of the war time, had given to the people on the Atlantic some idea of the sublimity of the Yosemite, and of the stateliness of the neighboring Sequoia Grove, that consideration was first given to the danger that such scenes might become private property and through the false taste, caprice or the requirements of some industrial speculation of their holders, their value to posterity be injured.

Yosemite has long been a place for mountaineering ascents. Today, rock climbing is a popular activity, using specialized equipment and techniques after careful training, for the granite walls of the park are among the world's finest for this sport.

State Geologist Josiah Whitney, also on the board of commissioners, agreed, and he was the first to use the phrase *national park,* applying it in 1868 to Yosemite. Others had used phrases such as "a grand national summer resort" (1867), and "the great American park of the Yosemite" (1868).

At that time the park was much smaller than it is today. It had but two small, separate pieces—

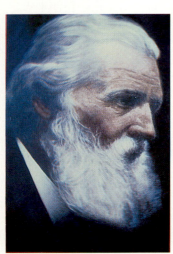

NPS PHOTO

John Muir, eminent naturalist of the nineteenth century, is often called "the father of Yosemite National Park" because of his tireless work and eloquent writings in its behalf.

the Yosemite Valley and the Mariposa Grove of Giant Sequoias. The watershed for the famous falls was still being grazed by sheep, and the High Sierra was still open to homesteading and mining claims. The problem of overgrazing was severe. In 1870 an astute observer, Professor Joseph LeConte of the University of California, recorded some 12,000 to 15,000 sheep in Tuolumne Meadows alone!

Fortunately, conservationists of the day saw the problem and rallied to correct the situation. More fortunately still, they had an eloquent spokesman in John Muir. Muir was new to California; he had not even arrived in the area until 1868, and then he spent his first year herding sheep in Yosemite's high pastures, including Tuolumne Meadows. (It was he who coined the term "hoofed locusts" for the devastating, woolly bundles.) But, even though he came late to the park cause, his firsthand experiences instilled in him a deep appreciation of the Yosemite region and of the problems it faced. When his publisher suggested launching a campaign to enlarge the park, Muir was immediately receptive.

Success was realized in 1890, when the park achieved substantially its present size, although some reductions occurred soon after in response to those who argued for the development of timber, mineral, grazing, and water resources. These reductions would certainly have grown throughout the years had it not been for the efforts of Muir and a group of university and other professional people from the San Francisco Bay area, people who foresaw that encroachment would continue if not met with solid resistance. Thus it was that in 1892 the Sierra Club was formed, with John Muir as its first president.

The only step then remaining was to place all parts of the park under one administration, the federal government. Action to accomplish this was started in 1903 by President Theodore Roosevelt following a camping trip to Glacier Point, a trip on which he was accompanied by Muir, the most persuasive supporter the park could have had. (Up to that time, the area had been administered by two entities: Yosemite Valley and the Mariposa Grove had remained under state management, through the old commission, and the surrounding area was administered by the Department of the Interior, which detailed army troops there for the purpose.) In 1906 the valley and Mariposa Grove were finally receded to the federal government and incorporated into the national park.

And so it is that Muir is sometimes called "the father of Yosemite National Park." Even though the initial park area was established several years before he first saw it and long before he began to work actively in its behalf, the accolade seems appropriate; Muir has been at least as influential in the development of the park idea as those who conceived it. His influence was felt in the legislative and executive halls of government, and his prolific writings (which require many pages just to list) made an important contribution to the cause of conservation not only in his day, but now as the nation once again emphasizes environmental concerns.

SUGGESTED READING

BUNNELL, LAFAYETTE H. *Discovery of the Yosemite—in 1851.* Reprint. Golden, Colo.: Outbooks, 1980.

HUTH, HANS. *Nature and the American: Three Centuries of Changing Attitudes.* Berkeley: Univ. of Calif., 1957.

HUTH, HANS. *Yosemite, the Story of an Idea.* Yosemite National Park: Yosemite Natural History Assn., 1964.

JONES, HOLWAY R. *John Muir and the Sierra Club: The Battle for Yosemite.* San Francisco: Sierra Club, 1965.

MUIR, JOHN. *Our Yosemite National Park.* Reprint. Golden, Colo.: Outbooks, 1980.

MUIR, JOHN. *The Proposed Yosemite National Park.* Reprint. Golden, Colo.: Outbooks, 1980.

RUSSELL, CARL P. *100 Years in Yosemite.* Yosemite National Park: Yosemite Natural History Assn., 1978.

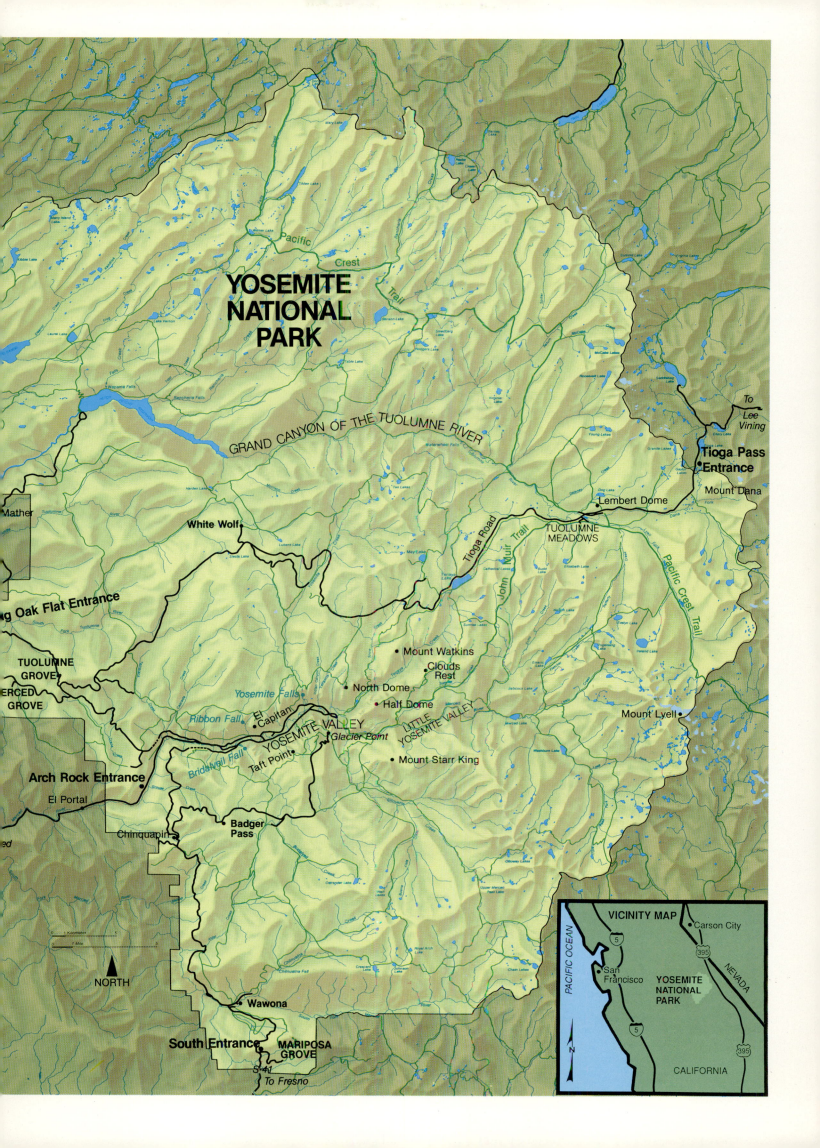

YOSEMITE
NATIONAL
PARK

Pacific

Crest

Trail

GRAND CANYON OF THE TUOLUMNE RIVER

To
Lee
Vining

**Tioga Pass
Entrance**

Mount Dana

Mather

Lembert Dome

White Wolf

Tioga Road

John Muir Trail

TUOLUMNE
MEADOWS

Pacific Crest Trail

g Oak Flat Entrance

**TUOLUMNE
GROVE**

**ERCED
GROVE**

ed

• Mount Watkins

Clouds
Rest

Yosemite Falls

• North Dome

Half Dome

LITTLE
YOSEMITE VALLEY

Mount Lyell •

Ribbon Fall

El
Capitan

YOSEMITE VALLEY

Glacier Point

Bridalveil Fall

Taft Point

• Mount Starr King

Arch Rock Entrance

El Portal

Chinquapin

**Badger
Pass**

NORTH

• Wawona

South Entrance   **MARIPOSA
GROVE**

To Fresno

VICINITY MAP

PACIFIC OCEAN

• Carson City

5

395

San
Francisco

YOSEMITE
NATIONAL
PARK

NEVADA

5

395

N

CALIFORNIA

Nature's Heritage

Already more than a century old, Yosemite has truly demonstrated its worth to Americans and to an increasing number of visitors from all over the world as well. For generations now it has been a vital part of our heritage. And as we are becoming more and more aware of the value—the *need* —for such islands of serenity in the modern world of ever-increasing industry and technology, the national-park concept is becoming more secure than ever. Indeed, it seems utterly inconceivable that such a wonderful region as Yosemite National Park could ever be put to any other use.

Those who enjoy a park such as Yosemite the most usually possess a rare and precious quality. Sometimes called "serendipity," this quality is the ability to discover something special in your surroundings, something you weren't looking for. Yosemite's treasures lie all around us, in plain view, just waiting to be noticed. Some are more obvious, such as Half Dome and the way the cliff face turns pink only at sunset. But others, such as Yosemite's nighttime denizens, her delicate wildflowers, and details such as the crystalline beauty of early-morning frost on grass, can easily go unnoticed in the shadow of Yosemite's spectacular features. These, and many, many more, are the treasures that lie in store for those who take the time to look and savor.

There is a story told in Yosemite that eloquently summarizes the appeal of the park and the infinite diversity of the wonders it contains: A lady visitor, who wanted to spend her time in Yosemite to the best advantage, asked a park ranger, "What would *you* do if you had only one day to spend in Yosemite?" "Madam," the ranger replied, "I'd weep."

> Climb the mountains and get their good tidings.
> Nature's peace will flow into you
>   as sunshine flows into trees.
> The winds will blow their own freshness into you,
>   and the storms their energy,
>   while cares will drop off like autumn leaves.
>
> —JOHN MUIR, *Our National Parks, 1901*

Sunset on Smedberg Lake in Yosemite's backcountry, a part of nature's heritage.

JOSEF MUENCH

Books in this series: Acadia, Alcatraz Island, Arches, Blue Ridge Parkway, Bryce Canyon, Canyon de Chelly, Canyonlands, Cape Cod, Capitol Reef, Channel Islands, Civil War Parks, Crater Lake, Death Valley, Denali, Dinosaur, Everglades, Fort Clatsop, Gettysburg, Glacier, Glen Canyon-Lake Powell, Grand Canyon, Grand Canyon-North Rim, Grand Teton, Great Smoky Mountains, Haleakala, Hawaii Volcanoes, Lake Mead-Hoover Dam, Lassen Volcanic, Lincoln Parks, Mount Rainier, Mount Rushmore, Mount St. Helens, National Park Service, National Seashores, North Cascades, Olympic, Pecos, Petrified Forest, Redwood, Rocky Mountain, Scotty's Castle, Sequoia-Kings Canyon, Shenandoah, Statue of Liberty, Theodore Roosevelt, Virgin Islands, Yellowstone, Yosemite, Zion.

Published by KC Publications · Box 14883 · Las Vegas, NV 89114

Inside back cover: The Giant's Stairway: Nevada and Vernal falls, Merced River. Photo by David Muench.
Back cover: People give scale to giant sequoias, Mariposa Grove. Photo by David Muench.

Printed by Dong-A Printing and Publishing, Seoul, Korea
Color Separations By Kwangyangsa Co., Ltd.